C000205053

Teach Your Cat
CORNISH

Funny & surprisingly clever books. Love. Love.
DAWN FRENCH, ACTOR & COMEDIAN

Anne Cakebread not only has the best name
in the universe, she has also come up with a
brilliantly funny book.
RICHARD HERRING, COMEDIAN

The cutest book I have ever seen in my life...
I'm supposed to be reviewing it and
then giving it back, but I'm afraid that's not
going to happen.
GAABRIEL BECKET, AMERICYMRU.NET

Teach Your Cat

CORNISH

Anne Cakebread

Thanks to:
Helen, Marcie, Lily, Fred and Wilma,
my family, friends and neighbours in
St Dogmaels for all their support and
encouragement, Carolyn at Y Lolfa
and Dr Talat Chaudhri for Cornish
translations and pronunciations.
Meur ras dhywgh.

In memory of Frieda, who started us on the
Teach Your Dog journey.

First impression: 2023

© Anne Cakebread & Y Lolfa Cyf., 2023

Illustrations and design by Anne Cakebread

ISBN: 978-1-80099-338-9

Published and printed in Wales on paper from well-maintained forests by
Y Lolfa Cyf., Talybont, Ceredigion SY24 5HE
e-mail ylolfa@ylolfa.com
website www.ylolfa.com
tel 01970 832 304

I grew up only speaking English.
When I moved to west Wales, I adopted Frieda,
a rescue whippet, who would only obey
Welsh commands.
Slowly, whilst dealing with Frieda, I realised that I was
overcoming my nerves about speaking Welsh aloud,
and my Welsh was improving as a result – this gave me
the idea of creating a series of books to help others
learn languages.
You don't even have to go abroad to practise.
If you haven't got a cat, any pet or soft toy
will do: just have fun learning and speaking
a new language.

– Anne Cakebread

Teach
Your Cat
Cornish

"Hello"

"Fatla genes"

pron:

"Fat-la gen-ez"

'ge'
as in
'get'

"Come here"

"Deus omma"

pron:
"D<u>u</u>hz <u>omma</u>"

'uh' as in '<u>u</u>rn'

rhymes with 'comma'

"Leave it!"

"Gas e!"

pron:
"Gahz e!"

'ah'
as in
'f**a**ther'

'e'
as in
'm**e**t'

"Stop!"

"Gortos!"

pron:

"Gore-toz!"

pronounce this 'r'

'o' as in 'hot'

"No!"

"Na!"

pron:
"N<u>a</u>h!"

'ah'
as in
'f<u>a</u>ther'

"Very good"

"Pur dha"

pron:

"Peer thah"

pronounce this 'r'

'th' as in 'this'

"How much is it?"

"Pygemmys
a gost?"

pron:

"Pee-gemiz a gost?"

'ge'
as in
'get'

'a'
as in
'ago'

'o'
as in
'hot'

"Don't scratch"

"Na wra kravas"

pron:

"N<u>a</u> rah <u>crav-a</u>z"

'a' as in '<u>ago</u>'

emphasise this syllable

'a' as in '<u>ago</u>'

"Are you OK?"

"Os ta
da lowr?"

pron:

"Oss ta dah low-r?"

'a'
as in
'ago'

pronounce
this
'r'

"Bedtime"

"Prys gweli"

pron:
"Preez gwell-ee"

"Goodnight"

"Nos da"

pron:

"Nawss dah"

'aw' as in 'awesome'

'ah' as in 'father'

"Be quiet!"

"Taw!"

pron:
"T<u>ow</u>!"

'ow'
as in
'c<u>ow</u>'

"Wake up!"

"Difun!"

pron:
"Dee-feen!"

"What's the time?"

"Py eur yw?"

pron:

"Pee <u>ur</u> yoo?"

'ur'
as in
'<u>urn</u>'

pronounce
this
'r'

"Lunchtime"

"Prys li"

pron:

"Preez lee"

"Are you full?"

"Os ta leun?"

pron:

"Oss ta luhn?"

'a'
as in
'ago'

'uh'
as in
'urn'

"All gone"

"Gyllys yw e"

pron:

"Gill-iz yoo e̱"

'e'
as in
'me̱t'

"What are you doing?"

"Pandra
wresta?"

pron:
"Pandra wrest-a?"

'a'
as in
'ago'

"It's snowing"

"Yma ergh ow kodha"

emphasise this syllable

pron:

"Uh-<u>mah</u> air owe <u>cotha</u>"

'co' as in '<u>cot</u>'

'th' as in '<u>this</u>'

pronounce this 'r'

"It's cold"

"Yeyn yw hi"

pron:

"Yain yoo hee"

'ain'
as in
'rain'

"It's hot"

"Pooth yw hi"

pron:
"Powth yoo hee"

'ow'
as in
'bowl'

'th'
as in
'thin'

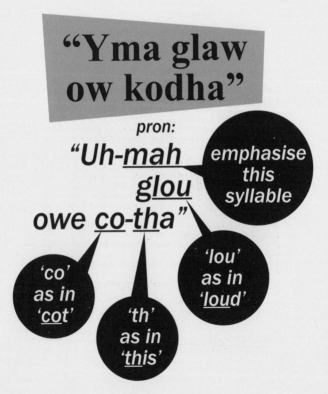

"It's windy"

"Gwynsek yw"

pron:
"Gwin-zek yoo"

"It's a nice day"

"Dydh da yw"

pron:

"Dee<u>th</u> dah yoo"

'th'
as in
'<u>th</u>is'

"Come down!"

"Deus yn-nans!"

pron:

"D<u>uh</u>z in-nanz!"

*'uh'
as in
'<u>u</u>rn'*

"Do you want to play?"

"A vyn'ta gwari?"

pron:

"A vin-ta gwaree?"

'A'
as in
'ago'

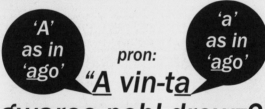

"What have you got?"

"Pandr'eus genes?"

pron:
"Pandruhz g<u>en</u>-ez?"

'ge'
as in
'g<u>et</u>'

“Where are you going?”

“Ple’th esta ow mos?”

‘eh’ as in ‘hair’

– but don’t pronounce the ‘r’

pron:

“Plehth ess-ta owe mawz?”

‘aw’ as in ‘awesome’

"What have
you been doing?"

"Pandra
veus'ta ow kul?"

pron:
"Pandra
vuhsta owe keel?"

"Have you got
a headache?"

"Eus drog
penn genes?"

pron:

"Uhz drawg
pen gen-ez?"

'ge'
as in
'get'

"Have you got tummy ache?"

"Eus drog torr genes?"

pron:

"Uhz drawg tor gen-ez?"

pronounce this 'r'

'ge' as in 'get'

"Have you got a cold?"

"Eus anwos genes?"

pron:

"Uhz ann-was gen-ez?"

'ge' as in 'get'

"Where are you?"

"Ple'th os ta?"

pron:

"Ple_h_th oss ta?"

'eh'
as in
'h_air_'
– but don't
pronounce
the 'r'

'a'
as in
'_a_go'

"Don't be afraid"

"Na vydh
own dhys"

pron:
"Na veeth own these"

'a'
as in
'man'

'th'
as in
'this'

"Get out!"

"Ke yn-mes!"

pron:

"K<u>eh</u> in-m<u>eh</u>z!"

'eh'
as in
'h<u>ai</u>r'
– but don't
pronounce
the 'r'

“Is that your favourite toy?”

“Dha degen dhrudh yw homma?”

‘Th’ as in ‘this’

‘e’ as in ‘met’

‘th’ as in ‘this’

pron:

“Tha dégen threeth yoo homma?”

"Do you want
a cuddle?"

"A vyn'ta
byrlans?"

pron:

"A vin-ta
beer-lanz?"

'A'
as in
'ago'

'a'
as in
'ago'

pronounce
this 'r'

"Cheers!"

"Yeghes!"

pron:
"Yay-hez!"

"I love you"

"My a'th kar"

pron:
"Mee <u>a</u>th ca<u>r</u>"

'a'
as in
'a<u>go</u>'

'th'
as in
'<u>th</u>in'

pronounce
this
'r'

"Happy Birthday"

"**Pennbloodh Lowen**"

pron:
"Pen-bl<u>ow</u>-<u>th</u>
Low-en"

'ow'
as in
'b<u>ow</u>l'

'th'
as in
'<u>th</u>is'

"Good luck"

"Chons da"

pron:
"Chonss dah"

'o'
as in
'hot'

"Merry Christmas"

"Nadelek Lowen"

pron:
"Na-dell-ek Low-en"

'a' as in 'man'

'e' as in 'met'

“Happy New Year”

“Bledhen Nowydh Dha dhys”

pron:

“Bleh-then Know-with Thah these”

‘th’ as in ‘this’

‘th’ as in ‘this’

"Thank you"

"Meur ras"

pron:
"Muhr rahss"

'uh'
as in
'urn'

'ah'
as in
'father'

pronounce
this 'r'

"How many?"

"Pygemmys?"

pron:

"Pee-gemiz?"

'ge'
as in
'get'

1
one

"onan"

pron:
"o-nen"

'o'
as in
'hot'

2
two

 "dew"

pron:
"de-w"

'e'
as in
'met'

'w'
as in
'cow'

3
three
"trí"

pron:
"tree"

4
four

"peswar"
pron:
"pez-wahr"

pronounce this 'r'

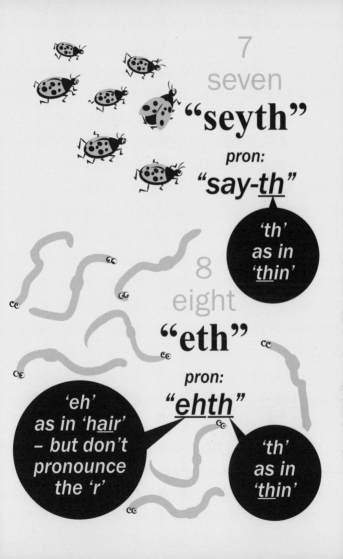

9
nine
"naw"
pron:
"now"

20
twenty

"ugens"

pron:

"ig-enz"

100
one hundred

"kans"

pron:

"canz"

"Are you happy?"

"Os ta lowen?"

pron:
"Oss ta low-en?"

'a'
as in
'ago'

"Have you got
enough room?"

"Eus lowr
a spas genes?"

pron:

*"Uhz low-r
a spa-ss gen-ez?"*

'a'
as in
'ago'

'ge'
as in
'get'

"Goodbye"

"Dyw genes"

pron:
"Dyoo gen-ez"

'ge'
as in
'get'